Contents

T0019877

1

Who is God?

To be a Catholic child in the 1940s and 1950s is to have been brought up on *The Baltimore Catechism Vol I-5*. This fragile little book of about 200 pages was the national Catholic catechism for children in the United States. It was enjoined by the Third Council of Baltimore in 1891 and based on Charles Bellarmine's *Small Catechism* written in 1614. Some of the most difficult questions in theology were reduced to question-answer format and shaped the basis of Catholic school theological education from the 1890s to at least the 1960s. Those answers ring through that generation – and me – to this day.

And yet, at the same time, I heard a story that signaled the end of such rote answers and universal perception. 'Computers are so powerful,' the story-teller declares, 'that pretty soon the country will be run by one computer, one man, and a dog.' 'Really?' says the hearer. 'How's that work?' 'Well,' the teller says, 'the man is there to feed the dog. And the dog is there to make sure the man doesn't touch the computer.'

Between the rote learning of catechetical surety and the computerisation of modern life lie two different kinds of learning, two different kinds of social development, two different ways of seeing life, and two completely distinct theologies of life. One of the models has all the answers before anyone asks the question; the second model has few, if any, universally held answers at all in a world where change is commonplace, yesterday is a vague memory and tomorrow is a work in progress.

In this current world, 'belief' is more an experience than an encyclopedia of data. It is reasoned, not recited.

Now, laughing at the improbability of non-human dominance over human rationality that the dog and the computer imply, are dying out. And with it, the *Baltimore Catechism*, as well. In fact, who would have thought? In one lifetime –

yours and mine – the world we expected to live in has all but totally disappeared.

We live from screen to screen now. Our children 'talk' to one another on their smart phones sitting across the room from each other instead of across their fences. Our cars run on electricity which means that gas and oil have suddenly become a liability rather than a miracle. Robots do our basic work and are about to become our closest companions. We talk across oceans to people we haven't really seen for years. We hold Zoom parties with the grand-children we have yet to meet in person. We shop in global bazaars on-line. We begin to save money for that first ticket to outer space. Some people have frozen their own bodies at death in expectation of their own resurrection as science gets closer and closer to extending life indefinitely.

But the way of doing business – on site or online – of raising families, all here or all somewhere else – and our sense of identity, biracial or intermarried or not – are not the only shifting stars on the human horizon these

11

days. God-talk – religious belief – has swung from hard right, as in we know the mind of God – to scattered leftisms, as in what mind of God? Yours, mine, or ours?

Mainstream churches, too, are reeling and rocking from challenges to ecclesiastical givens such as who may marry whom? Or why churches anyway? Or male-female genders – or not, of course. Then, in the face of new understandings of life and sex and gender an even bigger question: 'Who said so?'

Not surprisingly, in a time of massive global shifting of some very basic but very old principles, many ministers of many denominations are preaching to smaller congregations now. Some past believers have begun to look almost exclusively to science for truth they can count and touch rather than rules that now seem either lifeless or totally out of date.

Life has become more technological than human. More individual than communal. More independent than constrained by a universal conscience.

Deprived now of a common search for the meaning of life, secularism has emptied itself of faith, of hope even, and put in its place the worship of personal rights rather than communal or canonical responsibilities.

So then, what is there for me to believe in anymore? The answer is clear: Not what I once did, for sure – and yet, at the same time, I believe more now than I ever really understood. I began to see the loss of rainforests and the need for mountains as more meaningful than ministers preaching at us. Oceans and seashores, I could see, were more vulnerable than we. Classes and races of people, it became clear, were those whose lives were in our hands.

As seriously wrong as the divisions of society may be, the degrees of discomfort the outer limits of science may bring as we go on recklessly doing what can be done rather than determining what should be done, there is also an eternal reason for hope. After all, the dimensions of public power describe only our institutions. Not our people. Not our hearts. Not our souls. What public officials and institutions are doing wrong we can undo. If we ourselves are holy enough, committed enough, responsible enough to realise that the God we must believe in is the God who believes in us and relies on us to save this world.

We do still, in fact, have living models of the good life. Nurses who risked their own lives to save others from dying of COVID. Young people of all ages and ethnicities who protested police brutality and age-old racism marching night after night to wake up the rest of us. Leaders everywhere who took the helm of the country to maintain its democracy, to save its rainforests, to feed its starving children. They are the saints of our time.

Such as these spur us on to integrity, to generosity, to fullness of heart. And yet, many mourn the loss of a sense of common values and moral responsibilities, of the general acceptance of a Power beyond the power that comes with simply being alive and which once pointed all our hearts in the same direction.

Yet, I have also discovered that, as the

end of my life approaches, the purpose of the beginning years of life becomes more clear: Life is about coming gradually to the fullness of the moral self. Which leads of course to the basic question: What is that?

One thing for sure, the years have taught me that I really do not need things to grow me to the fullness of my real self. I don't need robots who sweep my floors to find happiness. I don't need to turn my life over to digital mysteries to assure me of the future. There is still something more important than all of that. It is the development of the self in the image of the God who made us so that what that God made we may return to the universe in even better condition.

The heart I have formed within me across the years is the measure of myself. It is in the attitudes I take to the civic enterprise – disdain or a commitment to the common good. It is the justice I seek not only for myself but for the poor as well, the compassion I have for immigrants lost in a sea of differences, the kind of leadership I seek in a world where money is more important than wisdom. Why? Because all of these are of our Creator God and are therefore my responsibility.

The problem is clear: There was a time when it was religion that was the Guardian of Hearts, that told us what to believe, that showed us how to act, that threatened us into the goodness of the time. But 'was', it appears now, was the operational term. So where is God now, who is God now, what does God want of me now?

In the light of these turns from the absolutes of a past time to the questions of this one, I have based this book on three basic questions from the *Baltimore Catechism*: 1. Who made me? 2. What must I do to gain heaven? 3. Why did God make me? Or to put it more succinctly now, how shall I know how to live in a world at the crossroad?

Ironically enough, while religion dims and even disappears from the scene in many cases, it is philosophy and psychology that hold out against the notion of giving up, of abandoning ourselves to the dregs of life. Of seeing it as useless. Of surrendering to its challenges, depressed by its losses and deluded by its fruitless promises of success, of wealth, of power, of whatever brings us to the brink.

Why? Because, instead of filling us with ease and comfort, psychology and philosophy confront us with the challenges of life, the effort it takes to become the best of ourselves, the reward of soul that comes with discovering that less is more and time is growth, and the awareness that we are not the end of creation but its beginning. We learn from them to reach beyond the reachable to the notion of a God so great, the presence of God so overwhelming that nothing we know of it here can possibly describe it. Nothing explains this life beyond Life. Nothing defines it, try as we dare. But everything draws us toward it.

It is out of a sense of the mysterious and the mighty, of creation and human community, that a new notion of God emerges in me. In the face of old but still extant models of God that were passed down to us, something even more impelling has taken me by the heart and drives me on to an awareness of something greater than the sum of all of them.

There are notions of God accrued across the generations that do more to destroy the idea of God than they do to seed it throughout the rational world. I know, because I had learned them all and none of them made sense.

God has always been a major question in my life. From early childhood on. As the years went by, I took what they taught me about God and tested all of them. God, the world around me insisted, was a magician, a puppeteer, a vending machine, a warrior, a tease. I struggled with every one of them. Decision: not one of them fit the bill.

God the Magician, I was to believe, made things happen that couldn't. Sun for the picnic on a rainy day, for instance, good grades for those who had not studied, full harvests for fields that got no water. If this were God, I thought, it couldn't be true that God loved everyone. Clearly, God had favorites.

God the Puppeteer pulled the strings of my life with merry abandon I was supposed to believe. But some people got jobs and money and gratuitous opportunities, I noticed, while others, equally or even more religious, got long-term illnesses that took away all the dreams of life. A few got money, of course, but most of the others were losers who watched the world pass them by. If this were God, I thought, this God was actually uncaring, uninterested in the likes of us. How could even the holy be ignored?

God the Vending Machine was powerful, yes, but not Just. A woman I knew went to church every Sunday to pray that her husband would stop drinking. But God was nowhere to be seen. She put in so many prayers and got out of all that devotion a divorce and three children to raise alone. It was the drunken husband who won that lottery. If this were God, I thought, the whole notion of what we said God wanted from us had to be wrong. Either we did not understand God at all or God was, at best, arbitrary, capricious, unreasonable – and testing us. Always testing us.

God the Warrior-Judge was even more

disturbing to me. A child of World War II, I prayed every day in school that God would defeat Germany, would crush the Japanese ... and, worst of all, in the end it seemed to me that God had 'heard our prayers'. But what did that mean: That God was punishing half the people of the globe who had nothing to do with plotting the wars that were killing them? But which half? Had God decided that the innocent of each nationality would simply be destroyed? Who of them had sinned? It was a question of profound ethical concern for me.

God the Tempter was even worse, even more disconcerting. God the Tease, it seemed to me, gave us Free Will and then watched us sin so we could be caught in the act and condemned forever.

I was already in the monastery when the implications of all that kind of theology, all these dimensions of 'God – taught so cavalierly, so casually – shook my faith to its foundations.

But then I remembered. Then, one thing saved me.

I was 13 years old when it happened. Late one night, early for our weekly Girl Scout meeting to start in the basement of the church, I decided – in Catholic terms – 'to make a visit' upstairs to the tabernacle where the communion hosts were kept from Mass to Mass.

I knelt at the communion rail in the deep darkness of the closed church and recited a few prayers – I don't really know which now – while the sanctuary candle, the one light in the great cavern of the Cathedral, flickered. I was completely alone. Then, suddenly, the tabernacle dissolved into bright light and poured into the nave. I was astonished. I had never seen anything like it before. Suspended in front of the tabernacle, it seemed, it magnetised me as I watched it slowly ebb away.

I got up off my knees – not afraid but fixed – and looked around. There was no one there. No janitor checking the lights. Nobody else making a late visit to church. I descended quietly to the basement. I had changed and I knew it. Somehow or other, the light was no longer outside of me. It was in me. I waited day after day for the Light within to go away, to fade, to end, to leave me. But it never has.

It was the year 2000 before I ever said a single word to anyone about that night. I was afraid people would think I made it up. After all, I was only 13. But that night changed my whole notion of the presence of God in our lives.

I have no doubt now that God is with us all and comes often to many in a burst of awareness. The difference is that the Presence becomes a guide, a warmth, not a vengeful human being writ large. Instead the cosmic God is a surety, a promise of support, a reminder of what the Jewish community has always called 'The Covenant' and the Quakers call 'The Inner Light'. God is the internal voice calling me to give myself to the fullness of life. It is the trek of the soul to wholeness and understanding. It is an awareness within me of my identity with all creation and the strength I need to wrestle my own uncertainty, indifference, spiritual deafness to the ground.

Let me explain: Science has become my spiritual director.

It is science that brought me face-to-face with the awareness of the overwhelming, immeasurable presence that is God. It took me to the edge of life, beyond the fairytale God. It helped me to understand that the Light was the energy from which all things come. It brought me to realise that the Cosmic Presence, the beginning and end of everything, has been consumed, dwarfed, shrunk, and reduced to magic, warring, vending, judging, and manipulating the laws of life.

God, to be God, is the substance, the embrace, the whole of life. It's out of five basic elements – oxygen, hydrogen, nitrogen, phosphorus and carbon – that all the elements of life come. These five elements are at the base of all life processes, in all of us, in all living things everywhere. 'We are made of the same makings as the stars,' Dr Ashley King, a planetary scientist and stardust expert teaches. 'Nearly all the elements in the human

23

body were made in a star...', and so, I believe, will return to stardust at the end.

The poets tell us that we are nothing but stardust. But stardust is the same stuff of a Cosmic God as we are its cosmic dust. Think of it: God is within us and we are within God, the Light – God, the energy of all life, God the Creator of the universe.

God within us is Light, the essence of revelation and insight. God within us is energy, the pointer toward the tomorrow that comes out of today. God within us pours out on us the reckless generation of the gifts of life.

But God is the mystery nobody wants. What people want from God is not mystery but certainty, the very element in ourselves that binds itself so often to making sure that nothing ever changes, that tomorrow never comes. Not because we are so sure that the Now is the acme of perfection but because we fear to let go of God's will for today in order to grow even greater ourselves by being willing to allow the new, the future, the possible to become. After 13 billion years of formation, it took our globe 4 billion years to develop to this point. The God of Time is the God we do not trust.

And so we shape God into a petty pretense of power – as magician, puppeteer, vending machine, warrior, judge and tease. In the hope of taming the procession of life, we spend life attempting to coax God to our whims. While all the time we pray for Trust.

What it comes down to is this, I decided: I can either believe in the greatness of God or not believe in God at all. But there is a price for that choice. Not to believe in the immensity of God in such an immense astral history is to believe only in myself and what I see around me. Without a God, I am God.

I make myself the god of my own world. I worship gods of my own making – money, power, prestige, approval, things and things and more things. I insist that I will worship nothing I cannot see, and so instead I worship all the things I do see, with all their limits, all their limitations, and all the limiting they do to the expanse of my soul. It is a sorry sight.

It is an even skimpier definition of humanity,

of myself. Without God, human dignity – my human dignity itself – is in danger. What else imbues human life with value, what else confers on a person an inalienable dignity, if not the fact that they, too, if there is a God, are more than they seem? That they are stardust, aglow in the dark and certain that they are not alone.

No God, no meaning. No God, no purpose. No God, no cosmic quality about us at all. We are simply sand flowing through a corruptible hourglass.

But I cannot go there. To watch a painter paint and a musician play a symphony of their own creation, and a poet capture in 200 words the meaning of life, and a writer break open beauty and reasoning and possibility and meaning and throw it into the night sky, a blessing wherever it falls, is to know that we are here as Words of God.

We are here to shout the name and praise the glory and trust the love that the Creator brings daily to us as creation. Then, we may make our own glories and give them recklessly away so that like stars breaking open and spewing more and more life and love, reason and care, knowing and wisdom into the air, is to understand that we are the stardust of the Creator and we are made to burn and light, to sparkle and shine, to be warmth and fearlessness as tonight fades into all the tomorrows of our lives.

The point is this: God, indeed, is a major theological problem, a major question. But God is a major answer, as well. Or otherwise, we would be left with no answer but ourselves. What a pity that would be.

The Sufi tell a story more penetrating than science, more profound than catechesis:

A Sufi on the way to the Mosque for the feastday had walked for days on the sand, in the heat. Then, with the minarets in view and sun streaming down on the dome, he said to himself, 'I have to rest a while' and sank to the ground.

He was hardly asleep until he felt a hard hand and heard a sharp tongue. The pilgrim over him was flailing his arms and shaking his head in disgust. 'What is the matter with you!'

he screamed at the Sufi. 'What kind of a Sufi are you? – Lying on the ground with your feet pointed at the holy place? Get up immediately.'

The Sufi smiled a bit, then opened one eye. 'Good Sir,' he smiled. 'I am grateful for your care and concern. Now, if you would be so good, could you turn my feet to where they would not be pointing at God.'

If at the end of my life, I go with God knowing that God and I are going together, I will know that God has indeed forever been with me, guiding me, holding me up, calling me on. The Presence of God is my theology now, not the niceties of religious prescriptions. What else is there, in fact?

2

What Must I Do to Gain Heaven?

THERE ARE TWO concepts, neither one of which taken alone is sufficient to explain what to do with our lives, but both of them together may give us a broader vision, a more pointed way to explain where we are as a people in this time and place in history.

The first commentary on life comes from Will Durant who writes, 'To give life meaning one must have a purpose greater than the self.'

A good heart, in other words, is a good gift. But it is not good enough to make life meaningful both for myself and for the time in which I live without content that tests its mettle and its integrity. The basic question becomes, then, is our theology all about me or all about us? The question challenges both our daily lives and our spiritual selves. A sense of purpose calls for great moral strength driven by a persistent commitment to the spirit of life rather than personal security and comfort. It means being committed to the evolution of creation rather than its exploitation.

The second insight comes from the teachings of Abba Anthony, a Desert Monastic who said to those who came out to his monastic cell seeking answers to the difficulties of life, 'The time is coming when people will be insane and when they see someone who is not insane they will attack that person saying: 'You are insane because you are not like us.'

Abba Anthony's insight is a warning not to accept the words of others without testing the truth of them ourselves. It is a call to risk being the other in the great debates of life, to invest in the questions of the time so that the future may be for all of us a clearer, softer road. A heart without a spine is at best the cultivation of a smiling face meant to distract the world as Rome burns rather than help put out the fire.

Both of those attitudes of mind – purpose and a sense of personal responsibility – test the theological depth of the times we all face now. A world without a sense of direction, a people without a conscious commitment to reason and rightness, to quality of life and character of purpose, shape both the culture of the nation and the ongoing dedication to life by the souls that guide it. Only then can we know if what we leave behind can possibly spur commitment to creation rather than commitment to the detritus of our so-called profit-making.

In fact, it's whether our theology is built on the wisdom of the ages or the willful wastage of life that will determine its quality from age to age. It will also cue us when to change it as one era outgrows another. Or how to understand it as it grows. Or which insanity we're facing at any given time: the narrowness of our own private theology and its spiritual blindness or the soul-charged call to new purpose as the Spirit strives to enliven one generation after another.

Meaning – purpose – is the engine of life. To know what we're doing and why we're doing it determines both the value and the global impact of our life's journey. A call to purpose is the pathfinder that leads us up one idea and down another until eventually we can get the journey right, make something of it, leave a path for others to find, and leave a legacy of conscience, as well. A sense of purpose is a reminder that the goal not only determines the journey but that it also leaves the route marked for others, too, to find their way, to build on what we've begun after we're no long here to carry it on.

As Abba Anthony teaches us, purpose is what underlies the kind of human journey that spends itself for something worth doing. One concern is to determine what drives it; the other is to save it from becoming shrunken, becoming absolute in a world in flux.

The second question from the *Baltimore Catechism*, then, prods us to think life's great theological questions through for ourselves before we set off on a trek through life with neither maps that show the way nor meaning enough to steer us. 'What shall we do to gain heaven?' the catechism asks each of us at a very basic age. It is the kind of compass-setting challenge that leads both the youngest and the oldest of us to ask what it is that we're meant to be about and why. Then the catechism points us true north and answers for us: we must 'praise Him, serve Him, and love Him'. But there is a problem built into the answer that itself belies the question.

It's at the juncture of growth and purpose that we begin to ferret out the many levels of meaning it takes to live a moral life. We begin to understand that the purpose of a moral life is to define morality, to embrace morality and to pursue it to the end – for all our sakes. Whatever the cost and the burden of it. For instance, here in a very standard answer – that too often rolls over our tongues and indeed our souls without a single protest – is a clear challenge to think things through all over again, wherever they come from. Even answers from the church and its catechisms.

We are, in the language of *The Baltimore Catechism*, taught to praise 'him'. To serve 'him'. To love 'him'. Our very notion of God becomes encased in maleness, that crown of creation. As if Godliness was maleness writ large. As a result, everything up to this era, it seems, is about half the answer to any question. It's always about 'him' and not 'them' or 'they' or 'her' or us. To pursue so narrow a question with so narrow an answer is to leave most of the world in want.

But few hear the dichotomy of it. The bias of it. The error of it. It has, in fact, taken centuries for us to even be allowed to raise the question of how it is that 'her' got moved into 'him' and all the 'he's' everywhere became the beginning and end of everything which leaves half the human race invisible, ineffective and ignored.

The notion that one person's needs or one group's demands can possibly bring us to a wholly correct answer is patently wrong, even misleading, certainly unjust. To pretend to relate to others as if they don't count can only leave us with a world in danger and our purpose obscured. And it has. We have been able to completely overlook the needs of the rest of the species and think we have done a good thing. Because we have overlooked the incompleteness of the question itself, we have no wisdom, no moral strength to bring to the problem of life or to the purpose of life.

The very first point of every question is to realise that every choice we make will leave another choice out. And what will we do about that then? Which means that there is in most all of our present responses to partial questions what itself breeds a kind of built-in insanity in the culture, in our lives. Not to see the whole prospective of anything that is encroaching on our lives is to wander fruitlessly through life, wanting to do something but unable to define what really must be done.

Which is why one of the other primary questions of the *The Baltimore Catechism*, after 'Who made me?', is 'What must I do to gain heaven?'. Unfortunately, the stock answer from *The Baltimore Catechism* itself left out a consciousness of anything but our own singular relationship with God – and leaves out as well the better part of the world

– which may be exactly why the answers it left us with are not working yet.

The answer, as it's phrased in the theology of an older era, simply leaves out the rest of the world, blinds us to it, and, I think, has left us in a world that is now reeling and raging from answers which until this time were always partial to begin with. So, where are we now and where are we going until we finally realise that only a theology of wholeness, of the interdependence of the entire human family, the responsibility to care for the planet and the understanding that humans are not the whole of creation but merely a part of creation can possibly save us? Or in this early language again, teach us 'how to gain heaven'? But that is a long and fragile time coming:

In 1967, Lynn White, Jr. wrote an essay that shook the social givens of the period and exposed the inability of the theology of the period to be any kind of gift to the modern world. White's insights, on the other hand, stretched the vision, even of the churches, to imagine a theology that took the whole globe, the whole planet, the entire earth itself into account and is now recognised as a classic statement of theological challenge.

'The major problem facing the modern world,' White argued in *The Historical Roots of our Ecological Crisis* is that the Judaeo-Christian ethic justifies domination.'

His thesis was a global one: 'What people do and fail to do about ecology-of-life issues depends,' he argued, 'on what people think about creation, think about themselves, and think about their relationship to things around them.'

It was a cry for the Judaeo-Christian world to stop talking about the grandeur of God in creation and begin to do something to live well in it. It was time to realise that, yes, God created the world ... but God did not finish it. That the Creator left for us to do. God left co-creation – ongoing development and fulfillment – to us. The purpose of each of our lives lies in maintaining creation, not destroying it. For ourselves? Of course. But for everyone and all of life to come, as well. It makes us morally responsible for the preservation of the globe. And in that we have been spiritually deficient in every possible way.

To really honor creation, we must begin to see the sacramentals of life in its grasses and rivers, its snowless mountain tops and dry river beds, its charred forests whose absence would affect the future of the country itself, its pollutants that would sicken babies from one side of the globe to the other, it's multiple peoples whose colors and ancestry have been left on the outside of the global community looking in.

Why was it happening? Because, White challenged the world to realise, our Western religious tradition teaches us to think human hierarchy, superiority, and domination.

The implications of a theology of domination built on scriptures that were interpreted by the modern world as a cornucopia of capitalist delights, a 'let-those-who-can-get-it-get-it' world, shook the foundations of an airy-fairy spiritual mythology that taught equality but gave the fruits of life only to those who fit the criteria of color, gender, class, and social status.

For the first time in history, however partial in its evaluation of the world-human relationship, with science in hand, analysts began to look to religious teachings for an understanding of the skew in the human-non human bond. For the first time, science sought to awaken spiritual attitudes of both praise for creation and repentance for having ignored the fact that the globe itself was being attacked by, of all things, the presence of humanity itself.

Worse, those who ignored it, polluted it, wasted it, and – often in the name of God – disdained and discounted its needs – were societies that wrote paeans to creation and did nothing to save it. Clearly, it was time for a new consciousness of the oneness of creation. It called for a new kind of commitment to creation, for an awareness of the rest of creation, rather than of our own selves only.

Lynn White was clear: the people who saw

themselves as the most spiritually committed on earth – Christians – by continuing to maintain some kind of moral division between matter and spirit were engineering the earth's demise. We all lived alone, saying prayers for ourselves, and taking the fruit of the land, the acreages of past forests, the endless fossil fuels to create a life-style of superabundance on one hand and destruction of the very things we needed on the other. Life immersed in this kind of theological certainty was life wrapped in errant incense where personal needs had become the purpose of its altars.

It was creation centered on humanity itself with no concern whatsoever that the resources it claimed for its benefit alone were also finite, not eternal, and as the scriptures read, were meant to be 'tilled and kept'.

Clearly, our 'purpose' has been ourselves alone.

In the end of this human drama, man [sic] became the acme of all life, its crown, its apogee glorified in every hymn and concerned with the redemption of humanity alone. But

42

most of all, it had it all, had everything, for its own service, its own use, its unrivaled personal interests. It was the setup for total destruction of everything to come. And we are clearly approaching that annihilation now.

Irony of ironies, the crown of creation – human beings, man [sic] – emerges from out of the earth to be God's agent, God's other self.

Most important of all, perhaps, is the notion that the last layer of the components of creation – humanity – is most momentous, most consequential of all. Greater than the universe. More lasting than the stars.

And in fact, what humanity has done to creation over time, is indeed consequential and now threatens time itself. We have drained marshlands, cleared forests, destroyed spawning areas and displaced animals everywhere – separating their habitats from their water with super highways, replacing their forest areas with cement jungles and in the end, ironically, jeopardising what we ourselves, as the top of the food chain,

43

need most. Everything else in creation is evaluated as lesser, secondary, derivative, disposable, without priority. God planned the world for human benefit, we insist. After all, the creation story says so: 'You, oh man,' Scripture reads, 'can have everything in the garden' to satisfy the unlimited desires of humankind while pollution circles the earth in eleven days.

It is only the second creation story that makes the link. The story of creation in Genesis 2, extends and deepens the human end of the creation story. In Genesis 2, God brings all the animals to Adam to be named – to be known, in other words, to be brought into relationship with humankind. As your pets are with you and my little parrot is with me. Why? Because by bringing the animals to the human for naming, the personal relationship between the two is demonstrated without doubt. Life, all life, these two kinds of life, are meant to be in relationship.

The human is not put into the garden to exploit the garden but to relate to it, to care for it, to be in conjunction with it, to become part of it. The 'common good', then must include all of creation, animals, flora, creatures of both land and sea, as well as humans. Not one need at the cost of the other.

Most damaging of all, of course, is the theological determination that humans are made in 'in God's image', and so are God's agents on earth. Free, autonomous, unrestrained – and responsible. In fact, it is exactly the awareness of that responsibility that is precisely the theology the human race must embrace if it and the rest of the world is to survive this theology of domination.

Genesis is clear. The fact of the matter is that, yes, God did create the world. But God did not complete it. God left the completion of that work up to us. And we are making a miserable disaster of it.

To deal with such insanity now is a matter of being willing to step outside the prevailing conspiracy theory, the ecological lie of the moment, the thought of lost support for non-human life that stops us. It is the thought of standing up in public and being different from the rest of the ideas in the room.

The basic question, the underlying question, becomes the more subtle line of thinking: Can I accept the burden of stepping outside the arc of social approval? Can I bear the responsibility of being ostracized by those whose intent is to draw a golden rope around those they approve of in society? Can I resist those who would exorcise those who do not fit the criteria of color, of social status, of belief, of need?

The point is that all creation is co-creation. What I choose to do or not do when I find myself face-to-face with the group mind is a crucial moment. It marks the depth of my understandings, the strength of my character, the quality of my heart. It is the moment Abba Anthony warns us about, the moment that all the others say of me, 'You are insane because you are not like us.'

For instance, Gaya Herrington's study of climate change data came out in 1972 – a mere five years after White's attempt to make religion aware of its moral responsibility for the damage to the globe. Herrington's work on the complementarity of any and all scientific studies of climate change up to that point, was a best seller. All of the data from all of the major climate research concurred: by the year 2040 if the United States stayed on the ecological road it was on, Western society as we knew it would collapse.

Co-signed by all the major scientists in the country, including those in the laboratories of the most prestigious of the offending corporations, the alert shook climatologists across the globe. Surely major change was on the way.

Instead, Big Gas and Big Oil spent millions of dollars, billions even, to undermine the numbers, to confuse the meaning of it all, to sow doubt in the minds of the people of the ecological impact of modern industry, pharmacology, mining and pollution, on who would be first and most harmed by climate change when it came. The black community in the ninth ward in New Orleans, for instance.

The forested homes in California that had been built right in the path of thousands of acres of forest fires, for instance. The oceans and the species in the oceans dying from the plastics and pollutants being dumped there.

But by attacking the data, corporate America – confused by the scientific readings, overwhelmed by the implications of the date, moved on in the same directions they'd been plying for decades and created even more damage. Until now.

When Gaya Herrington, freed of daily work and locked down in COVID-America updated her findings from 1972 to now, with California burning and New York and New Jersey flooding in September of 2020, it became clear. There was only one error in the climate data of 1972: the climate collapse was raging on at an even faster pace than expected. Cultural collapse was doomed now, not for 2040 but for 2020 – twenty years sooner than Herrington's official data had concluded in 1972.

The bond between humanity and the rest of creation was snapping. Animal species were disappearing at an ever-increasing rate. With the loss of mountain snow, rivers were drying up from coast to coast. Shorelines were eroding and consuming the high-end wealthy communities that had built to the edges everywhere. Farmlands lacked irrigation while cities flooded, crops were stunted, and, finally, solar panels were selling out. Late, years too late, but selling. Human superiority had gone as far it could go, it seemed.

The Theology of Co-creation, completing the work that God has begun but left to us to finish, is, apparently, no stronger in its repentance or recommitment now than it has ever been. Missing Mass on Sunday is still ranked a mortal sin in the theology books. Using fossil fuels to increase a company's profiteering is not. In fact, it is not mentioned at all.

We – our political leaders, our corporations, our 'strategic planners' – have apparently planned no future strategies beyond repeating the old ones, the ones that have for so long simply ignored the theology of co-creation in favor of the worn-out theology of domination that had seduced the industrial-technological world to its peril. And yet, nothing is really changing - certainly not the leadership we need to provide the spiritual attitudes and theology of purpose the world seeks right now.

Instead, parliaments and congresses refuse to face the fact that the money we need to confront the tornado of destruction we have built up over these last decades may be our last chance to continue the work of co-creation that the scriptures meant for us to embrace.

My Theology of purpose is a clear and creation-oriented one: unless and until humanity, all of us, begin to see our purpose as embracing the call to co-create the world in the face of its demise, there soon will not be one worth saving.

Reliance on the doctrine of human superiority has run its course. Whatever theology of co-creation can be rescued from the shards of fire and water, bad air and polluted soil must rise now. Immediately. If it's not already too late to resurrect what had been left to us to begin with.

Durant got it right: 'To give life meaning, we must have a purpose, a theology, larger than ourselves.' Or, as Abba Anthony told us, those who called the heralds of climate change insane may will be found to be the most of the insanely irreligious themselves. Then what will we all say about what we need to do to gain heaven?

3

Why Did God Make Us?

ANOTHER QUESTION THE *Baltimore Catechism* confronted us with was an important one. It asks us, 'Why did God make us?' The answer was worth the price of the book. 'God made us,' the catechism promised, 'to show forth His goodness and to share with us His everlasting happiness in heaven.' The message we memorised as children about God was an uplifting one.

At the same time, two small stories have pulled at my heart – let alone my theology – for years now. They tell me something about the place and valuation of women that not only has a universal ring of recognition to it, but a painful one as well.

In the first story, a young woman asks, 'Old woman, what is the most difficult thing a woman has to bear in life?' And the old woman answers, 'The most difficult burden a woman has in life, dear, is having no burden to bear at all.'

The answer sends a twinge down my spine to this day. Who runs the country? Men – and notice what is happening to it. Who runs the church? Men – and see how people have been fleeing it? Who is the invisible servant in the room? The Women – untried, untested, uneducated or over-educated for what they are expected, permitted, to do in society but who are made to do what church and state define for them.

It is a long, tired history of hidden women in every generation, every society, who have broken through the wall, ignored the social blockages to become themselves, and so graced the nation and the world with ability then denied but not confirmed by science itself.

These were the women who were often ignored during their lifetime and only 'discovered' later, when they were long dead and could do no public harm to the divine order of things. They were the exceptions to humanity, the work of many of them even claimed by the men who denied them their own identity. Their hidden existence became the strange pieces of folklore whispered from generation to generation. They were the vestiges of hope suppressed. They are The Original Sin of the male world that confined them to child-bearing, to the physical tasks of domestic life, to the raising of sons and daughters to fight the next war. They had no burden to bear beyond the burden of being suppressed, being ignored, being demeaned, being unseen.

Apparently the most important question of all – Are women human? – was never asked. Instead, the myth of female weakness, mental deficiency, and emotional inadequacy went virtually unassailed for centuries.

The second story is at least as depressing – and demanding of change – as the first.

A rug merchant in the Middle East went from bazaar to bazaar in search of new rug patterns to take back for sale in his own country. Suddenly, he saw a masterpiece hanging in an empty stall that was being operated by an old woman sitting cross-legged on the ground, counting her beads, and praying.

The merchant pulled up his horse abruptly and shouted, 'Old Lady, how much for the rug hanging behind you?' She never moved but called back, 'A hundred rupees, Sir.'

The merchant was astounded. 'A hundred rupees?!' The woman straightened her back a bit, 'Yes, sir,' she shouted back. 'A hundred rupees and not a single rupee less.'

The Merchant shifted in the saddle. 'But old woman, if you know that this is a valuable rug why are you selling it for only a hundred rupees?'

This time he saw the woman frown a bit, her head lower, her shoulders slump. 'I am selling this rug for a hundred rupees, Sir, because I never knew that there were numbers above a hundred ...'

End of universal story in a world which, the churchmen say, 'God made us to show forth God's goodness and to share God's everlasting happiness....' So, what happened to that 'sharing' for women and how is that affecting all of us yet?

Answer: Mightily.

We have ignored half the human resources of the world, women. We have, in other words, limited the development of half the human race. We have ignored a bank of resources that are badly needed in a world that is now technical, digital, coded, and basically male in its strategic planning and decision-making. A world which, as a result, is deteriorating right before our eyes.

While the male world produced automobiles, steam engines, light bulbs, repeater rifles, tanks, armies, gas stoves, telephones and nuclear bombs, no one even noticed that women had been overlooked. No, not 'overlooked'. They had, in fact, simply been refused, denied, banned in their attempts to be fully human.

Hard as it is to believe, in the light of the historical time-line of the modern world, it was not until 1952 that 'the woman's question' became an international question, an item on the agenda of the new brand new international political hub, the United Nations. Together

Eleanor Roosevelt and President John F. Kennedy managed to put women, the other half of humanity, on the official agenda of the human race. A miracle, indeed.

Women whose needs, talents, insights, wisdom and intelligence, had until this time been stolidly ignored as full and functioning human beings had suddenly appeared on the international agenda. Of the 193 countries in the world, after two world wars and the great experiment of nuclear annihilation, 99 countries signed the first document on human rights for women and pledged themselves to accord full humanity to the women of the world. Almost 50 other countries and 2 non-members of the United Nations, Palestine and the Vatican, did not commit themselves to such bold and dangerous 'sharing of goods ... happiness of life' to women.

Were women really capable of functioning independently of male overseers, of male thinkers, of male superintendency. And what would happen to the support men enjoyed once women decided for themselves how those benefits were to be distributed.

To both church and state, human rights were a male thing.

The primitive notion was that men were the life-givers and women simply nourishing receptacles of the male seed in much the same manner that the farm land around them received the farmer's seed and brought forth a harvest.

Medieval Roman Catholic Scholastics wove elaborate arguments to explain that man by virtue of this life-giving potential, was spirit, was reason, was power 'in the image of God' but that woman was carnal, emotional and passive. 'Woman is secondary both in purpose (sex) and in material (body)' Thomas Aquinas said. 'This has the negative effect on her moral discernment.' Her ability, in other words, to make decisions, to spot truth was nil. Quite literally, then, man would have to be her head.

A thousand years of that kind of teaching cannot be gainsaid. And so the church closed its schools, universities and seminaries to girls and women far into the twentieth century.

Family life was preached under the heading of the father but not a single word was ever said about wife-beating being a sin and the mother a mere service center for it. Even church language is almost exclusively male: about God -'Him', about 'dear brothers', male pronouns in hymns and prayers, about boys but not girls on the altar 'unless no men or boys are available', the new versions read. Yet, there's not a word about the lack of authentication for the ministries of women as catechists or pastoral associates, let alone the deaconesses they refuse to depute despite their commonplace in the church up to the fourteenth century. All these simple things the church needs to do if women are ever to feel truly present in the church. Truly welcome there. Truly important to the religion of Jesus, who told the woman first that he was the Messiah.

And while they're at it, an encyclical on Gender Equality in the Church would be a good start.

Until those things happen, it will take decades to erase the effect of John

Chrysostom's curse, 'Among all savage beasts none is found so harmful as women' or Thomas Aquinas' even more negative dictum, 'Woman is an occasional and incomplete being,' he decreed ... 'a misbegotten male. It is unchangeable that woman is destined to live under man's influence and has no authority from her Lord.'

And so, without the church to lead them as it should have, the member states of the United Nations moved on to address the greatest question of them all: Did all human beings, whatever their state of mind and life, really have the right to human rights?

In answer, the nations of the world bound themselves to protecting the fullness of humanity for women as well as for men; the Catholic church, however, made no such statement and did not join in the ownership of this one—the implication being that God wanted women to live under male superintendency.

But Church or no church, human rights for women as well as for men has become the holy grail of women everywhere. While an international body oversees the treatment of women as a requirement of their membership in the United Nations, its ten basic human rights are miles away from being common to women everywhere. The effects of all of them linger in the hearts of those who wanted the Church to lead but watched the State do it instead.

Before World War II it was not commonplace for a woman to own property – because she was a woman. She could not assume a debt without her husband's permission because she was a woman. She could not get a job without the permission of her husband because she was a woman. She could not support herself on her own skills and quality because she was a woman. She could not quit the marriage without complex and costly proof of abandonment or abuse. She could not get into many colleges or their departments – medicine, law, finance, psychiatry, surgery, urology, veterinary science, until the mid-nineteenth century. In 1968, some states were still not admitting women to jury duty on the grounds that 'women were too sentimental' to sit on a jury.

Then, the United Nations in its Declaration of Human Rights and associated documents outlined 30 human rights applicable to all human beings. Of these, ten were closest to the daily lives of women: 1. the right to life; 2. the right to freedom from torture and inhumane treatment; 3. The right to equal treatment before the law; 4. The right to privacy; 5. The right to asylum; 6. The right to marry and have family; 7. The right to freedom of thought, religion, opinion and expression; 8. The right to work; 9. The right to education; 10. The right to social services.

According to the United Nations some progress has been made, yes, but the problem lies in the fear of recession anywhere, everywhere. And just as serious, these goals go on being considered under the purview of men rather than inalienable human rights which no man has the right to refuse.

The effects of the diminishment of women

are catastrophic. In a village in India a few months ago, girls' schools were burned down. Several years ago, the kidnapping of hundreds of girls in Africa as sex slaves for soldiers was commonplace. Limitations on girls in Afghanistan have been reinstated.

Everywhere, the right of women to determine their own life-paths have been violated – one way or another – as at least 200 million women and girls between 15-19 in 30 countries have undergone FGM. Female genital mutilation is meant to make sex painful so that women are unlikely to seek male companionship other than the relationships to which they have been bound.

The very notion of women leaders is rejected – even in the West – though research everywhere confirms the fact that companies that have female leaders show 30 per cent more profit than those that don't and that though women leaders and male leaders have different styles and goals both are necessary. According to *Forbes* magazine, as of February 2012, 119 nations had never had a female head of state or head of government, including the United States.

In 18 countries, husbands can legally prevent their wives from working. Some 49 countries lack laws protecting women from domestic violence. The implications are clear: women who cannot earn money independently can never become independent of violent men.

Women have made important inroads into political office but after all these years their representation in national parliaments where the laws are made that affect women most are 24-30 per cent, still far from parity.

Decisions about sexual relations, contraceptive use and health care often lie outside a woman's purview whether married or not.

Movements to protect women and girls from underage marriage, abandonment and death is yet unachieved while thousands of girls live at the mercy of lustful old men, rampaging soldiers, and kidnappers everywhere.

The European Union (EU) and the United Nations (UN) are embarking on a new, global, multi-year program - the Spotlight Initiative - focused on elimination all forms of violence against women and girls.

And yet, now, at this moment, femicide is a plague in Mexico.

Women's job market participation has been stagnating for the last 25 years as home child care now costs more than rent and mortgages. More than 100 countries committed to advance gender equality for women and girls everywhere during the UN General Assembly in New York in October 2020.

The full development of women, I'm sure, will take the efforts, the teaching, the model, the ongoing understanding that the Woman's Question is not a woman's question. It is a human question and none of us will be wholly human until we each demand the need to share God's goodness and happiness with women as well as claim it for men. Because, beware, there are women everywhere who are learning that there are numbers above a hundred for them, too.

What is my theology of God's will for us on

earth? My theology rests on one thing I'm sure of, on one thing I know: the church itself will not be fully Christian, fully faithful, fully holy until it realises that the woman's question is the very question on which its own holiness will be judged.

In summary

I HAVE GROWN beyond a list of theological questions and answers. My God is the essence of life; my purpose rests in God's call to our responsibility for co-creation; and the equality of women is my measure of the authenticity religion – any religion – claims as theological validity.

Appendix:
My final declaration
of belief

Taken from *Illuminated Life* (Orbis Books, 2000). Used with permission.

Amma Syncletica said: 'In the beginning, there is struggle and a lot of work for those who come near to God. But after that, there is indescribable joy. It is just like building a fire: at first it's smoky and your eyes water, but later you get the desired result. Thus we ought to light the divine fire in ourselves with tears and effort.'

The important thing to remember in the spiritual life is that religion is a means, not an end. When we stop at the level of the rules and the laws, the doctrines and the dogmas – good guides as these may be – and call those things the spiritual life, we have stopped far short of the meaning of life, the call of the divine, the fullness of the self.

Enlightenment is the ability to see beyond all the things we make God to find God. We make religion God, and so fail to see godliness where religion is not, though goodness is clear and constant in the simplest of people, the remotest of places. We make national honor God, and fail to see the presence of God in other nations, particularly non-Christian nations. We make personal security God, and fail to see God in the bleak and barren dimensions of life. We make our own human color the color of God, and fail to see God in the one who comes in different guise.

We give God gender and miss the spirit of God everywhere in everyone. We separate spirit and matter as if they were two different things, though we know now from quantum physics that matter is simply fields of force made dense by the spirit of Energy. We are one with the Universe, in other words. We are not separate from it or different from it. We are not above it. We are in it, all of us and everything, swimming in an energy that is God. To be enlightened is to see behind the forms to the God who holds them in being.

Enlightenment sees, too, beyond the shapes and icons that intend to personalise God to the God that is too personal, too encompassing, to be any one shape or form or name. Enlightenment takes us beyond our parochialisms to the presence of God everywhere, in everyone, in the universe.

To be enlightened is to be in touch with the God within and around us more than it is to be engulfed in any single way, any one manifestation, any specific denominational or nationalistic construct, however good and well-intentioned it may be.

It is a practice in many monasteries to turn and bow to the sister walking in procession with you after bowing to the altar as you enter chapel for prayer. The meaning of such a monastic custom is clear: God is as much in the world around us, as much in one another, as on that altar or in that chapel. God is the stuff of our lives, the breath of our very souls, calling us always to a heightened understanding of Life in all its forms.

To be enlightened is to know that heaven is

79

not 'coming'. Heaven is here. We have simply not been able to realise that yet because, like King Arthur and his search for the Holy Grail, we look in all the wrong places, worship all the wrong idols, get fixated on all the wrong notions of God. We are always on our way to somewhere else when this place, the place in which I stand, wherever it is, is the place of my procession into God, the site of my union with the Life that gives life.

To be contemplative I must put down my notions of separateness from God and let God speak to me through everything that seeps through the universe into the pores of my minuscule little life. Then I will find myself, as Amma Syncletica promises, at the flash point of the divine fire.